The Fastening
by Julie Doxsee

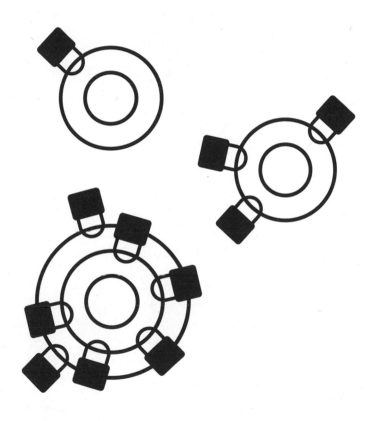

also by Julie Doxsee

Objects for a Fog Death (2010)
The Next Monsters (2013)
What Replaces Us When We Go (2018)

Black Ocean
P.O. Box 52030
Boston, MA 02205
blackocean.org

ISBN: 978-1-939568-49-6

Library of Congress Control Number: 2021953185

FIRST EDITION

For my true loves my sons

Contents

I

II

III

IV

V

is it you, the bubble given back to the air
without its silver skin?

— René Daumal trans. Pierre Joris

I.

HOYRAN

Among the ruins was a staircase to nowhere
roaring turquoise into the sky.
When you peeled the orange
bought from a nomad on the coast
I could see your mouth fade around it
like your tongue could make anything
liquefy. I was aware under my feet
were rocks harder than any surface
I'd moved over, each step
a mallet to my gong-skull
seizing the fat buoyancy
that kept me graceful. At night
these rocks led us to a tomb
where we lit a fire in a dint
at the top of a grave
and cooked a fish over it.
How many falling stars did you see
as we pulled the fish apart with our fingers
in the star-cut dark?
I saw one meteroid
grow big like a fast-waxing
moon coming toward us
as though we were flecked
with locked-in laser dots, ready to lose
it all. I saw it turn to stardust

in seconds flat. You and I
were never there ever
in the liquid night, crook-necked,
prepping to explode, were we?
I remember my feet
all cut up as we left the tomb-field,
dragging toward the VW
wedged between
two bleached ruins. You told me
time doesn't mean anything
when your speed-of-light
is just a rhyme embedded
in soaking pages. The hard rock,
the wet wood, fish bones we left
for bats. I did throw
my poems into the sea and walk to
the bus stop. I did ride a bus
further and further inland
till my hands found a cold
doorknob to wrap around.
The sea; the sea can infect you. The
moonrise over it, the gritty skin it leaves.
I don't remember. I don't remember
any small part of the truth with you
but I felt the rocks and how
they cut me and still I
walk over them every single day.

THORN STAB

A xylem holding my lover
by the wrist corkscrews
all the way up his arm.
His cigarette cloud
stops short, blunt
lassoed. He stabs his finger
like Rilke plodding gently
over velvet petals, snagged.
Did you know Rilke, the poet
who breathed numinous acres
of ferver into the brown land, died
from a thorn stab? Veins
of red infection forked fast
onto his porcelain limbs
and sprinted into his heart like
a thousand harpoons.
His mother raised him a girl,
bundling bouquets in his cute dresses
digging earth with trimmed claws
free as a whip in the garden acres.
My lover's blood darkens
the roof garden.

Tomatoes, peppers, phlox,
raspberries, cold ivy splashed
with ink-blood. It looks nothing
like shadows. It looks sturdier
than ink. It's wet
like a river, not like messy
death-terror. Painting his
hands in the zip-zip
dusk, some vampiric genie re-awakes.

UNPACK

When the house decayed, I drove
around for days, messy swerves
in the foothills. I stared
at my foot on the brake,
swallowed by machine-tomb. I couldn't
get out and lie on the grass—
it was grave and grey with snowman
slush. I couldn't swim under the snow-floor
feeling the prophecy creep. Prophecy,
I can't love you. Prophecy,
the future is rattling.

THE SEEDS

There are possibilities in bailing.
You can go to Spain. You can
tear down your trailer and plant
a cactus field. Put on a blue helmet
and scale down a glacial rock
that takes one whole year to get
to the bottom of. Be careful.
There is a poem about eating an apple
by digging your thumbs into it
bit by bit till you get past the seeds.
What does your rappel
down the final feet
hold for you? It could be
a whole suspension of you
for the time it takes
to bury someone deep
into your skin and wriggle
them into place, past the
labyrinthine veins and bones
that cage someone up
and tango someone around
till they squish into
a shape you made inside
your nerves. You can't

dig your thumbs into the moon
and climb back up. Hunger is
elastic seeds. Hunger is this.
Hunger has no cure, it
comes back and back to
eat you. Take your microphone
off. Take your clothes off, take
your mouth and teeth off
and try to feed
your whole anatomy.

FALL SCENE WITH TRACKS

She heard the truck horns
and the weather was sleety.
That night the river
was a proud mother
full of reedy swishes
like babies committing
reverse suicide:
joy-i-rise, laugh-i-try.
This is the story of when
people got too old
to confess their sadness
and said, instead, things like:
It is easy to walk forward
and walk forward again
but easier to lie down
in the harkening light of the
train whistle, the gravel
track. No, not near it
or on it. Don't think
of pancaked, gutted bodies
with blackened wheel-rails
paralleling the pelvis and
sternum. Near in imagination—
the strobing mono-light
blurring as it wails near.

SCENE II

From a bed, a dream
is the numbing blanket
where you pretend
a sponge the size of you
sucks the air out for a minute
and plants it back
after throwing it into a tornado
for a minute. This kind of
purification is okay.
We all live with very very
big dirt. Gravel in the veins
and things. We also live with
little dirt, juddering and jolting
when we cough. Do you cry out?
This might be a death scene—
do you cry? It may not be
a death scene. I don't
have my story together.
But I have memory foam
when I feel weighty
enough to wisp into
nonchalance, smiling calm.
By then it won't be too late
for the curve of the spine

to parenthesize the twists
of air left and right. Oh, air.
Oh, baby. These days are golden
in their perversity,
outwardly blowing wide
and returning.

THE FASTENING

Cluttered with poem-clothes
I see nothing. In winter
your hands strip my tights
to the ankles, slinking me
over the sanctum. In this corner
I could gather the magic V
at the base of my shirt and throw it
into your mouth, wetting everything.
But I can't see anything this night.
I can't see the red eels
of your pistol grip
pressing my pearly thighs.
I can't feel gravity
and the dead logs
it made of my legs—
stalks frozen wide, waiting.
I feel you crowd my body
in a tinged hug, a thud
pulsing slow behind the throat.
My ribs are electrocuted wood
in chemical pools never surfacing.

Month after month I see nothing.
The crowding, the thud.
It's raw. My heart ate a whale.
I love you.
I spend Fall catching objects
on fire with my eyes.
It is a question of tethering
daylight to the match, a little pine stick
impregnated with chemicals
made to save poor women
from death. You. The sunup
from a far, far pinnacle.
I still love you. Still.
I go out into the night
to look for little animals
that survived. The beams of
their little red eyes. Two houses go up
on my block. A third and fourth.
I notice yards overheaped
with logs, unattended—
low branches igniting in wind.
You will end up in my survival show
about this. You will be
the person who hugs me hardest
when we're all sent home.

CRACKED

I fall in love
down to the bone,
the 206 bones
humanly countable.
Very divisible. Very singular
in form, and from
my single sacrum
lightning leaks by
electric finger. Like,
my Zoom job
on this shock plateau
zaps. Unzips. Skyrockets.
I can show you
my heap of cracked remains
charring coldly.
But let's examine
the full, wobbling heart
of the electric man,
siphoning blood
from the 6-foot body
back into itself,
aortic balloon
vacuuming his
bear-form flat;

and I selfishly want
to send orgasms
into the stratosphere.
There are people
who know what I mean.
Someone died on me once
and caverns of
former loves
got together to mourn,
shrieking on the floor
in our coal costumes
while men around us
went whoa. I stayed under
my bourbon coat
in a corner of the empty house
till raw-gray; inside-out.
There were little sculptures
in our freezer
but there was
nothing I would think
to thaw: A little ice-cube cabin,
a little candy robot. An igloo
made of fig chops. What kind
of poet leaves her flesh-twin
out there, dying. Faring.
I have everything to say
now that the metal

will crack his chest
then drown
then own him—
the hospital air
a gritty math of slit skin
and cracks and a heart
outside the body, like a little
skinned bunny on the curb.
All of this is totally nuts.

II.

CRATERS

Every seventh month
hedonists try to place
their bodies in the path
of all nine planets
as they orbit
the I love you.

This is because hedonists
know an orbit
is a slow burn
not a boulder-slam
that would shake
all hungry nerves
so patiently alive.

You may disagree but
the feel of rough stones
on skin is better than
a mud-hug and better than
twisted slips of
mariner-grade knottings
up and down the body
forcing
the heart back into
its tight container.

You can't unstir a pot.
You can rub yourself
against the side of a planet's
gaseous craters and feel
the drunken swirls
and gashing stabs
grinding into your skin,
mixing with all those lumps
in your chest, mixing
the loud sounds and
head-washed slanting
of a perfect scream
stuck in the middle of
your roughed-out throat.

When a body is a soft
sketch, it is so very
easy to coax up
a mountain, so very
light like a perfect, milky
pillow; so very nice
to sleep all the way inside of
till the meteors strike.

BANGKOK

I enjoy phases of time
like that. I once enjoyed
a goat hoof in the heart,
kicking hard. Still, I have
skin-aches boring out and out
and out to the smothering
bricks. Am I taller than you?
The mountains in Bangkok
were steep from the taller
side. I want to visit
falling monastery walls—
visit some hoof prints
softly kicking the coast
like a chronology roaming
the calendar, the island path.
In sign language a year is
a clenched hand with a loose
hand enwrapping it.
Two years is the same loose
hand more loosened by
twin-taut fingers and a slacker
enwrapping. Three years,
three slackenings. Enwrapping,
unfolding. I'm not scared

of this neighborhood,
nor of the way hands show pause,
maps, the finger-limit of five.
We started this way—in words
and in the shit they do,
reaching to enfold the small animals
that were our hearts. Do you see
the first and last of us, the number
we go to? A friend died and I
wanted to stay in his inbox
after that—to stay with all the
alive people, too, a beacon
waving nonstop from a peak.
You talk with hands
tied back or lifting to move
words like him or her or
us in and up and folded
together in radial light.
I like that a heart exceeds
an armspan, that hands can hold
sudden voltage to twirl around
and admire in the cloud-light—
changing underneath and above
and against whoever we are.

THE BEAKS

I tried to read your book and it was tight
and sanitary, and because I am drunk
and loose, I found the sentences
about buckled-up dresses and
diamond-lit tea rooms
hard to breathe within.
I don't like going to the theater and
I don't like reading text messages
that come in green bubbles.
I'm stupid. There are very few places
on earth for me to breathe when
my heart hurts. Windows show
unturned stones and I don't care.
Let them hatch worms. Let the worms
feed beaks: big beaks and baby beaks. Beaks of
the sparrow and beaks of the grouse
and the beaks of the flailing, cut chickens
spurting into the air so bloody and close-faced.
I wanted this. I wanted to paint everything
in wonderful, wet leaks. Thick, smoothable
radii. I wanted more viscosity on
my fingertips so I could measure
the ways your sex body would
spill and spill and spill. And now

I will spell it out: When you decide
it's time to choke me I will take
my green clawed scarf of chicken-foot
voodoo from around my neck and
let you see the blood-diamond
holes in my skin. You can dig
into the blood and make it leak
more and put it wherever
you want. This would be
romantic. Put my blood in your
ear, in your mouth, in your own
precisely-laddered arm slashes—
and our blood will mix and spill
into the ground, emptying us
all the way till we wake up
inflated and gorgeous and fluid
like sealed-up rooms.

BANG EMOJI

It isn't that there's no
honesty out there. It's just
that storylines have always
discreeted themselves
into tree hollows, followers,
phoneys, mannequin-ruins.
There's always a ruin in my
gut when I feel tidal waves coming
on—stubborn gulfs that
once felt [bang emoji]
then sprouted tentacles with
their suction pods and
brain-hunger. I don't want
a time machine that asks me
to bury my long-ago heart
into a fine silt on the luke-warm
mountain. Only the believers
know or think or know or think
new hearts will sprout
with glorious storylines
that branch into the many
fake heavens and the many fake
roadways that artists can't
fake. Where do I put

my sideways questions and
why? Why do people think it's
bad to be cracked out
of a shell and balled up
on a cold floor? A cold floor
can stab you alive in super-sweet
ways! A cold floor can be
the brace cracking your spine
without making your eyes
bleed. From a cold floor you can
look to the ceiling to see
the blood fan out like
a carnation you never wanted
to see blown apart but
now that you see it blown
apart you know, at least,
to trace the wound
from the thickest gathering
of red outward: to where it lightens,
gets so faint, and fades.

MAPS ARE YOU

I complimented you, saying
women must love you
because you are all maps and
good voodoo and you are
anchored to gallery owners
that let you live in their galleries
to make crunchy, crashing art.
They let you summon
the high-collared goat men
who bring cherries and
grapes to serve in wood bowls
as you drift off
in the Texas star-fog
of big gallery windows.

I told you about my student
who wrote a poem thanking
his shooter for the bullet
in his rib because without a
bullet in his rib he wouldn't
feel emotions or be in college.
You said: I am more mess than map
though I care very deeply about
all shot flesh and the bullet-dotted
bones I just woke up in.
I care about all the
damns and shits that collapse me.

You called yourself part of
of the masculine scourge:
the gunless scourge
needing castration regardless.

You said you were going far off
on a dirt road onto a far off
mountain to find the right
scissors for the removal.

Maps, I said. You
are all maps and maps are you
and that's why women
love you and trace you
from here to dirty mountains.
That's why women chase bears
toward you; to see
the sublime awe-face your
eyebrows make when
a live bear comes close
to give you a kill hug. Is that
the kind of hug a bear would give?
What kind of hug would a bear
give? A whole-body chomp?
Well, that's why women bare their
claws and stir your shot-glass
with an index tip and let you
lick the whiskey off.

III.

10,000 GLINTS

When I am touched
on the shoulder
my hand flings zeros
that rip forth into the
blackness out there.
There is a whole lot
of windy noise when
a sudden face comes
to kiss me in the recess.
A witness saw
this pair of hands
part my lips
from outside-in
and freeze there,
awaiting exhale
and the boundary
of my cold body.
Thank you, thank you for
this other breathing body
and the slaps of wind-breath
in my ears, but
who in this muddy wild
has joined me?
A hand used to close

around my face, covering it
like a nerve, like
a switching limit, like
all you need is hands.
All you need is hands.

PLANET GRAVEL

I was awake all night
scrubbed of wires
and of the ribbons of veins
that used to pump
good blood around.
Mosaic flesh parts
head to toe, unpieced,
cracks blackening apart.
I ideated scrubbing
the planet gravel
with steel wool
to raw the commotion,
sheen it tender. The word
tender means kind and
loving and caring.
It means money
and pain and juicy.
How did thrall
wholly evaporate
then precipitate
me tight inside
a shucked shell

shaped just like
my body but more
lashed? I look for
baby teeth
lost in the backyard
grass-acres.
Until I find them I think
my children are dreams:
stereo mist-flesh
expanding loud
into the hollows
of the house.
I note
the spaces between
each raindrop on the window,
able to analyze
the convectional soak, the degree
of saturation I would step into
beyond container-walls
right out the front door
and into the echo-echo
of a clean foot-pace
all the way to the sea.

But they'll be
6-feet tall one day
learning how

human tentacles
can reach so far
into another
person to
scrub them out.
I was awake
all night—
each clawed-up
skin fiber
knotted
into one giant
heart; my whole body
a raw heart
radiating to the bottom
of my gut.
Have you ever
felt that? What keeps
you safe, human?
Have you ever felt
like you
swallowed a whale?

IV.

MASTERPIECE OF THE HIJACKED GIRL

The strobe noise, the twisting knob
and heavy synth. A small river town
with farms and silos and a few
trimmed bushes, but. There are
tables full of comet-red beverages
and bad divorce haze. There
are hobbies, too, and my secret
superpower scrawled in graphite
inside a pink diary kept at
my father's house. Now's your shot
his friend said. Be a poet, just stay
out of trouble. Don't be the boiling over
of your own buzzing skin.
When I'm old enough, I'll know
a mother's sunset can't blacken out
the underside of the door, I'll know
I can't stay by the river in the park
because there's no protection
from being a girl. Not from the
scouts, not from the normal-looking hands
that turn evil doorknobs, or normal
doorknobs under evil, turning hands.

You suck up to my talent.
Pretend I am good.
I carry everything I do with me
wherever I go and you follow. I put all
the dirt you want into my poems
so you can put your body all over them.
I don't know; what do you want.
You can't take my body unless you
unbox my book and box up your
skin-fringed, boiling hands.
And when I pretend to be elsewhere
I know I am a Masterpiece and here
is the cover: It is a photo of a chair
exploding to pieces in the fog.

I write a play and star as the lead.
It's a lot to memorize. I pick
your costume out too but you're not
in the play so why did I do that
and what are you doing in my head.
Wear this, then leave. And leave
me alone. The fabric is thin;
I see where your bumps flare out
like a sudden scream, slap, blast, zap, cramp.
I want to be a writer and a good one.
I wear my talent like a blazing, fucking
scab. Layers of shelled-over blood-armor
line the hallways and the balustrades of
the grand tier in my opera house,
mezzanine flooded with mold stench
and shit-screams; wormy boils and grease.
I told you I hate diamond-lit ballrooms.
You bloat me with the servile histrionics
of foreshortened champagne with
paralytic sham-stuns that come
from your fingertips
and laser eyes. I want to say fuck off
because I know who you are
and who all of you are
who slip into hallways to
invisibly tie the rotted carrot
to the dangle-wand
then dangle and dangle.

My Mom wouldn't like you
and wouldn't like to see you
outside my window with that slick
masquerade mask and those
golden pants and shoes. She would
bloodlet you and wretch up
her midnight sandwich if she knew.

There is a new reality. The real
binds of ropes on my ankles.
My hands. I didn't know you tore up
my play after closing night.
You drug and drive me
far far from my Mom in a blue
Subaru. I want to say fuck you. I know
what is happening but I ask you what is
happening. And you knife my ropes off
1000 miles away in Mexico
or Houston in a room
with palm tree wallpaper. Please
don't do this to me, to the limits
of the old landline, the faint-scrawled
paper of my girl voice:
police, police, police.

V.

VILLAGE BREAKFAST

A woman in a black headscarf
said to me "You
looked in the mirror
when you were pregnant
and your blood got plugged
deep into your babies."
She smiled. I ordered village breakfast.
I watched her light coals
to make my food. I watched
small people bring chopped vegetables
and oils to her as she rolled dough
onto the cast iron.
She was pretty. I held my
babies and rooted them
like kangaroos into my chest,
watermarking them forever.
Here are some features: The tight
feel of colors I forgot
folded over bones, reflecting
mercury-blue. I have no
clue what my name is here
or was there, rough forms of me

caroming up the branch tips,
sap exploding, metallic beads
raining into the skin
warm and little in my hands.

THE ODYL

Her eyes took it
all the way to the next village
where the churches cooled it.
When she, eight,
fingered the flashbulb,
a little round sunup
mothering mini-planets iced her.
The churches with black
velvet walls, and churches
with worn-out Marys
crying chipped paint,
all of those churches stoning
the wide shriek of open sun
and the unpressed hollow
of her electric bones.
She removed lint from
a bird nest in the street
and pocketed it, eggs long
hatched or bashed.
She tried kissing upward
into the sky that feeling

she always felt
she was lugging toward—
whitish-bluish shrill
rattling in the open.

BLACKOUT

I was dark, bundled,
hovering tissues over water
as snow dwindled
all panic it made when mounds
entombed slid cars, slid time
to dark buffers the other
world wouldn't see. It's not here,
the house key on a string, bait
to pop light and jolt the town.
A melt is a balance of matter,
a subtraction and a traction.
Inhales subtracted from exhales
equal zero, so death takes the most
plus and minus, the most ache and
calculate. And ache. Snow on the grid
blows black around, ice mountains
go back to the sky when they stop
annoying and clogging and killing.
It's dark here where keys don't blaze
because keys are not. Lightning's
whims of power lock spare percentages
of light in the freeform, little fires
in a coal sea. It's cold. It's night.
I've and they've failed my frozen

babies. I look to the furthest hill where
nothing is my fault. I look to the
animal eyes and dead tree line. I look
to the moon's tomb where everything
is a mystic whiteout so my body
can shake this debt.

GRAND HOTEL DE LONDRES

I forgot, in the shriek of
clouds, you smoke.
Our balcony costars
two naked statues
and the subzero sea
in diamond light
and us fogging breath
over night-glow granite.
The million people
on the street
look up to hail
two stone people
(they think they feel
hot stars fly out and
form and form and
jolt a million fevers alive—
and they do, they feel
from their night tombs
and their diamond
eyes a new pulse).
From our balcony
I didn't see your face, then
I did, then a million
whole years looped

into our poet blood,
our shrieking smoke-faces,
and froze them raw.
We're older. The world
brings us to burn
and keeps bringing us.

Author Notes

Hoyran is an ancient city of Lycian ruins from 1300 BC, featuring many ancient sarcophagi overlooking the Mediterranean Sea. As of my last visit in 2019, ten years after I met and traveled with the father-of-my-children through Hoyran and surrounding Lycian villages, the only sign indicating Hoyran's whereabouts, still, is a small hand-painted sign on a rock in orange-ish yellow with an orange-ish yellow arrow pointing south. The walk to the sarcophagi involves wandering through a small village of ancient still-inhabited stone houses beyond which is a tomb field on a vista a few hundred meters above the sea.

I left Turkey in 2016 with my children under desperate circumstances involving political tensions, financial stress, ubiquitous security and safety concerns from terrorist organizations, and—affecting it all—relationship precariousness. Some of the healing from exchanging one existence for another is reflected in the work.

Writing most of this book in Pennsylvania after I left Turkey and before the pandemic, then finalizing it during lockdown, helped me to untangle some unhealthy entanglements. Unentangled, I realize beauty reveals itself in particular ways for the poet that are unattainable for the real me, and vice versa. Reality-me cannot process beauty without Poet and Poet has no idea what love is despite attempts to dissect every molecule of it. I am thankful for how words expose the rawness of love while simultaneously watering it down enough for human survival. I wouldn't have a heartbeat without this paradox.

Acknowledgements

Deep thank yous to:

Andrew Wessels who moved to Istanbul after a long poemless period in my early-motherhood years, then read some early versions of some of the poems in this manuscript.

Bin Ramke for the story of Rilke.

The late Jack Gilbert's poem "Hunger" for inspiring "The Seeds."

Mathias Svalina, an eternal source of friendship and inspiration to the poetry community, who read some early versions of poems in this manuscript. I also thank him for MAPS.

Greg Murray, whose *Muse /A Journal* published an earlier version of "Grand Hotel de Londres."

Anna McMurray for late-night stories and wise friendship— here, there, far, virtual, collegial, forever—and through airing out every single high and low of these pandemic years.

Zachary Schomburg for including "Unpack" in OCTO 2.

Marc Luker, whose friendship inspired "Bangkok."

Elizabeth Gonzalez and Maxine Faulk who know how to raise good men while hosting resuscitative virtual happy hours.

Susan Knoll and Erik Anderson for their intelligence, friendship, and infinite support in PA.

J'Lyn Chapman for knowing me beneath the stars at Hoyran.

Maria James-Thiaw for always existing as capital-P Poet.

Janaka Stucky, Carrie Oliva Adams and the Black Ocean family for professionalism and supporting my work for the past twelve years.

Julie Doxsee is a Canadian-American author of five books of poetry. She holds a PhD in English and Creative Writing from the University of Denver and an MFA in Writing from the School of the Art Institute of Chicago. Upon repatriating to the states after nine years in Turkey, she moved to Pennsylvania in 2016.